CREATE -AN- AUTOBIOGRAPHY

WRITING A PERSONAL STORY

Me and my best friend

My first pet

My Life

Written by Eleanor W. Hoomes, Ph.D
Text Illustrated by Karen Neulinger
Cover Illustrated by James Uttel

ACKNOWLEDGEMENTS

I wish to thank all the English students and gifted students that I have taught in Heard County, Georgia, and Carroll County, Georgia, from 1963-1985. The activities in *Create-An-Autobiography* were all field-tested with those students and frequently revised as a result of their reactions.

Thank you, Former Students!

ISBN 0-56644-000-9

© Eleanor Wolfe Hoomes, Ph.D., 1986
Second Edition, Revised: 1995

EDUCATIONAL IMPRESSIONS, INC.
Hawthorne, New Jersey 07507

Contents

Introduction to the Teacher

Students like to create, write, and share stories; however, they can be baffled and become resentful when told to write a short story without being shown how to write one. Not knowing where nor how to begin, much less how to develop and end, they often write one skimpy paragraph and call it a short story. Conversely, when they are led through the structure of a story, step by step, they often surprise even themselves with the results.

Wise teachers of writing begin with what is already familiar and interesting to students and use that interest as a springboard to introduce new material. *Create-an-Autobiography: Writing a Personal Story* builds on the existing interest that students already have in themselves and their lives. It is natural for students, as for most humans, to have an interest in telling about their ventures, problems, and interests.

Very often young students' first creative-writing experiences are based on the subject they know best—themselves. As students grow older, they continue to enjoy writing about themselves. It is surprising how analytical some can become and how well they understand themselves. On the other hand, some students do not see themselves the way others see them. Some older students, especially those who do not have the so-called "perfect" home life, may have a tendency to gloss over or misrepresent perceived unpleasant situations in order to appear more "normal." Some shy students may find autobiographical writing difficult because they feel self-conscious about revealing their private thoughts, ideas, and life experiences. Guided by a sensitive and mature teacher, these students can greatly benefit from autobiographical writing. They can be led to understand themselves and their worlds better.

Children can write—some better than others, of course—but they all have the raw materials needed for creative writing floating around in their lives. *Create-an-Autobiography* is designed to bring order to those raw materials, help students sort and arrange that which is already familiar, and use the results to create stories. *Create-an-Autobiography* may be used in conjunction with a unit on autobiographical and biographical literature, or it may be used in a personal discovery unit. With only a few modifications, it can be used with grades 4-12.

Create-an-Autobiography will help develop students' abilities in observing, concluding, understanding, recalling, applying, analyzing, synthesizing, evaluating, and divergent and convergent thinking. At the same time it will contribute to the development of their oral, written, and imaginative skills, with the additional advantage of being fun. And finally, it can give students an end product of which they will be proud.

The unit is designed to save thinking and preparation time for teachers and to encourage planned creativity. Some teachers neither need nor want minute descriptions of teaching approaches and objectives while other teachers, because of time limitations, need more detailed instructions. All are capable of modifying an idea to suit their own purposes and most prefer to innovate rather than copy. Therefore, teachers may use *Create-an-Autobiography* any way they wish, with only their imaginations limiting the various possibilities.

I hope that *Create-an-Autobiography* will be as educational and as much fun for other teachers and students as it was for my students and me. If you and your students enjoy using *Create-an-Autobiography,* you might like to examine other books in the Create-a-Story Series: *Create-a-Sleuth, Create-a-Monster, Create Heroes and Villains, Create-a-Future, Create-a-Fantasy, Create-a-Utopia,* and *Create-a-Comedy*. Ask for them at your favorite teachers' store or write to Educational Impressions at the following address: 210 Sixth Avenue, Hawthorne, NJ 07507-0077.

Good luck!

Eleanor Wolfe Hoomes

NOTE: To increase the ease of use of this book, a duplicate set of student worksheet pages is provided. These perforated pages, which appear at the back of the book, may be detached for photocopying for use by the buyer in the classroom. This allows the teacher to keep the set of Teacher Directions and Student Pages together in the book.

PART I:
Past
and
Present

Past and Present

Activities 1 through 15

Teacher Directions

Objectives: To encourage and guide students to write by using their own lives as resources

To help students understand themselves better

Thinking Skills: Observation

Recall

Understanding

Application

Analysis

Divergent Thinking

Convergent Thinking

Synthesis

Evaluation

Directions: Activities 1 through 15 require students to write about their past and present lives.

Activities 1 through 7 demand factual information; however, creativity, and especially humor, should be encouraged.

Activity 8 requires some ordering of experiences to achieve interesting writing. The use of hyperbole to bolster humor could be introduced here.

Activities 9 through 14 start with the concrete but combine some fantasy and imagination with the concrete for interesting results. Create a comfortable atmosphere so students will feel free to be "themselves."

Activity 15 encourages students to start the practice of writing journals and/or diaries.

Past and Present

Additional Information:

To be good writers students must become good observers and listeners. They must learn to see, hear, feel, taste, and smell with all five senses, as well as with their minds and their imaginations. They should learn to take note of the little things that happen around them—the way a friend's mouth quirks to one side when she is stifling a giggle, the way another friend's voice moves an octave higher when he talks to a pretty girl, the way a dog greets his owner, how a cat's fur feels, how cinnamon smells . . .

Students should learn to utilize their stored memories to recall past experiences—disappointments, joys, sorrows, dreams, aspirations, emotions, feelings, reactions. In recalling and analyzing these experiences they should also evaluate them to determine whether they have value and/or interest so that others may enjoy, appreciate, or benefit from them.

Students should learn that sometimes the most trivial events can be developed so that they both teach and entertain, especially if the writer's reaction is one commonly shared by others.

Most important of all is the development of trust and respect between teacher and students. If students feel accepted and comfortable in the classroom, they will be more willing and eager to open up and share with their classmates and teacher.

The Past and The Present

Directions for Writing About Personal Experiences

1. Tell enough at the beginning to identify the subject, but do not get bogged down in too many minute details;

2. Observe carefully; record accurately;

3. Recall from memory vivid impressions and minute details that add spice and authenticity;

4. Decide the meaning or importance an experience has for you, the writer;

5. Decide what reaction(s) you wish to evoke from your audience;

6. With the meaning of the experience and the desired reader reaction clearly in mind, select the details;

7. Arrange and develop the details in an orderly, logical, meaningful manner;

8. Be honest—don't cover or hide or discard (unless it is necessary for "tightness");

9. Avoid unnecessary modifiers; instead, use vivid, specific words. Use metaphors, similes, hyperbole, and other figures of speech; and

10. Tie everything together at the end, but don't overexplain. The ending should be complete and strong.

Mirror Image

Very few people know what they really look like to other people. In the following exercise you will describe yourself, starting at the top of your head and ending with your feet. You will need a full-length mirror and a hand mirror. Recent photographs may also be used. You may **not** ask anyone for help—you must determine the color of your hair, the color of your eyes, and the shape of your face yourself. Some characteristics are measurable; some will require a value judgment.

Name _____ Age _____ Sex _____

Height_____ Weight_____ Body Build_____

Hair Color _____ Texture _____ Style _____

Face Shape _____ Eye Color _____ Skin Color_____

Eyebrows _____ Nose _____ Mouth _____ Ears _____

Hand Shape _____ Ring Size _____ Fingernails _____

Arms _____ Legs _____

Foot Size _____ Shape _____

Distinguishing Marks _____

_____

Other Comments_____

_____

_____

What do you like best about your looks? Why?

_____

_____

_____

What do you like least about your looks? Why?

_____

_____

_____

Personality

Activity No. 2

What kind of personality do you have? Use the following set of questions as a guide to get you started; then add your own questions. You may use friends and family members to help you.

What kind of disposition do you have?

_____

_____

_____

What is your favorite time of day—the part of the day when you are most alert and productive and you feel the best?

_____

_____

How do you handle problems?

_____

_____

_____

Do you like a lot of friends or a few good ones? Explain.

_____

_____

_____

Do you like to work alone or with others? Explain.

_____

_____

_____

How do you get along with younger people? With older people? With your peers?

_____

_____

_____

Personality

What are your favorite activities? Explain.

_____

_____

_____

What peculiar traits, habits, or gestures are common to you?

_____

_____

_____

Do you have any phobias? If so, explain.

_____

_____

_____

What kind of speech do you use? Do you use slang? Explain. Do you have an accent? Explain.

_____

_____

_____

Are you the kind of person who likes to be independent, to do things your own way and at your own pace, or are you a ''crowd follower,'' one who goes along with whatever else the others want to do? Explain your answer.

_____

_____

_____

Other comments:

_____

_____

_____

Interview

In this activity you will interview yourself. First, read interviews and watch interviews on television. Notice how the best interviewers ask leading questions to direct their interviewees but allow the interviewees to do the majority of the talking. Also, notice how good interviewers are able to change focus or direction when the situation demands it. Second, answer the following questions: How could you make the interviews you read and watched better? What questions were not asked to which you wanted to know the answers? Third, construct your own questions, making them interesting and probing. Fourth, answer your questions thoroughly.

_____

_____

_____

_____

_____

_____

_____

_____

_____

_____

_____

_____

_____

_____

_____

_____

_____

A Typical Day

So nothing ever happens to you, and you never have anything to write about? Hah! Don't you believe it. This activity will show you that in the normal course of a day things do happen that you can write about. Has today, so far, been a fairly typical day in your life? In this activity, you will write about **today.** Start at the beginning and work through the day detail by detail in chronological order, including where you went, what you ate, how you dressed, whom you saw, what was done, how you felt, and your reactions and thoughts.

A TYPICAL DAY IN MY LIFE

_____

_____

_____

_____

_____

_____

_____

_____

_____

_____

_____

_____

_____

_____

_____

_____

Famous Firsts

People seem to remember their ''firsts.'' Choose one of the ''firsts'' listed below, or supply your own ''first'' and write a story about it.

My first party

My first birthday

My first Christmas

My first phone call

My first punishment

My first love

My first day of school

Other firsts: _____

_____

My first haircut

My first bicycle ride alone

My first date

My first pay check (or allowance)

My first visit to the dentist

My first visit to a restaurant

My first night away from home

Other firsts: _____

_____

MY FIRST _____

_____

_____

_____

_____

_____

_____

_____

_____

_____

_____

_____

_____

_____

After School

What is your favorite after-school activity? What do you enjoy doing the most on weekends and after school is out during the week? In the space below, write a description of this activity (or activities) and tell why you enjoy it (them).

MY FAVORITE AFTER-SCHOOL ACTIVITY

_____

_____

_____

_____

_____

_____

_____

_____

_____

_____

_____

_____

_____

_____

_____

_____

_____

_____

_____

_____

When I Was Little

What was your life like when you were "little," before you started to go to school? How did you view the world? What were some misconceptions you had? What was a typical day like? What were your favorite games, toys, or people? You may need to interview others for some background information. If so, work the interview(s) into your account.

WHEN I WAS LITTLE

_____

_____

_____

_____

_____

_____

_____

_____

_____

_____

_____

_____

_____

_____

_____

_____

_____

_____

_____

_____

Anecdotes

An anecdote is a short narrative of an interesting, amusing, and/or biographical incident. Refer to any issue of *Reader's Digest* and read "Humor in Uniform" or "Life in These United States" for examples of anecdotes. Analyze several anecdotes by answering the following questions: What do the anecdotes have in common? Why are they interesting and/or amusing? How is the humor achieved? How are the anecdotes different? Which is your favorite? Why? After you have analyzed several anecdotes, write your own. Remember, anecdotes are brief and to the point; however, you must include enough details so that your anecdote makes sense.

_____

_____

_____

_____

_____

_____

_____

_____

_____

_____

_____

_____

_____

_____

_____

_____

_____

Wanted Posters

Choose one or more of the following and design wanted posters for them:

My ideal teacher	*My ideal parents*
My ideal school	*My ideal best friend*
My ideal pet	*My ideal sibling*
My ideal neighbors	*My ideal neighborhood*
My ideal house or room	*My ideal food*
My ideal environment	*My ideal day*
My ideal vacation	*My ideal trip*
Other ideals: _____	*Other ideals:* _____

_____   _____

_____   _____

WANTED: MY IDEAL _____   **WANTED: MY IDEAL _____**

Superstitions

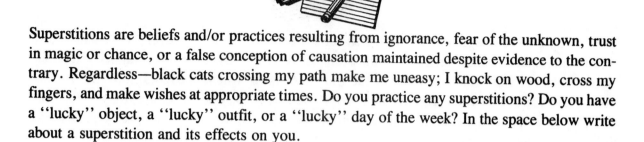

Superstitions are beliefs and/or practices resulting from ignorance, fear of the unknown, trust in magic or chance, or a false conception of causation maintained despite evidence to the contrary. Regardless—black cats crossing my path make me uneasy; I knock on wood, cross my fingers, and make wishes at appropriate times. Do you practice any superstitions? Do you have a ''lucky'' object, a ''lucky'' outfit, or a ''lucky'' day of the week? In the space below write about a superstition and its effects on you.

MY SUPERSTITION

_____

_____

_____

_____

_____

_____

_____

_____

_____

_____

_____

_____

_____

_____

_____

_____

_____

_____

Imaginary Friends

Many people have imaginary friends when they are very young; however, one of the most famous imaginary friends belonged to an adult. Elwood P. Dowd and his imaginary six-foot rabbit, Harvey, were made famous in the movie *Harvey,* which starred Jimmy Stewart as Dowd. Did you (or do you still) have imaginary friends? If so, who were (are) they? What did (do) they do? What happened to them if you no longer have them? In the space below write about your imaginary friend(s).

MY IMAGINARY FRIEND(S)

_____

_____

_____

_____

_____

_____

_____

_____

_____

_____

_____

_____

_____

_____

_____

_____

_____

_____

_____

_____

If...

In this activity you are going to imaginatively remove all restraints in your life and let your creativity determine what your life would be like if you could live anywhere you wanted, be anything you wanted, and do anything you wanted, whenever you wanted—well, you get the drift, I'm sure. So, give it a try.

If I could live anywhere and any way I wanted, I would _____

_____

_____

_____

_____

_____

If I could be anything I wanted, I would _____

_____

_____

_____

_____

_____

_____

If I could do anything I wanted, whenever I wanted, I would _____

_____

_____

_____

_____

_____

_____

Create-an-Autobiography 23

Role Reversal

What would it be like for you to change places with someone for a while? In Mark Twain's *The Prince and the Pauper* the prince and the pauper changed places for a time. In Mary Rodgers' *Freaky Friday* a mother and a daughter changed personalities. In *The Whipping Boy* the prince and his whipping boy were mistaken for each other. What would happen if you became your teacher, your parent, your dog, or your best friend? Choose something or someone you would like to be for a short period of time. Write about what would happen and how you would feel if you could reverse roles.

WHEN I SWITCHED ROLES WITH _____

_____

_____

_____

_____

_____

_____

_____

_____

_____

_____

_____

_____

_____

_____

_____

_____

_____

_____

_____

And the Winner Is...

You have just won $50,000 on a game show. The $50,000 must be spent within a twenty-four-hour period. It cannot be saved or invested. How will you spend your money?

MONEY TO SPEND

_____

_____

_____

_____

_____

_____

_____

_____

_____

_____

_____

_____

_____

_____

_____

_____

_____

_____

_____

Journals and Diaries

You can create your own written history by keeping a journal or a diary. A journal or a diary is an account of events, transactions, or observations or a record of experiences, ideas, or reflections kept regularly for private use. Journal or diary entries should always be dated with the day, the month, and the year given. The place of writing should also be noted. You can purchase diaries and journals or you can make your own using notebooks. Many writers prefer to use loose-leaf notebooks because they can make the entries as long as they wish in them.

Start to keep a diary or journal. Be sure to write about typical days and events as well as unusual ones. You will probably want to include some of the topics listed below.

Where I go

What I do

Whom I see

What I say

What they say

How I feel about _____

My reaction(s) to _____

Plans

Current events

What's popular in music, dance, dress, slang, TV, movies, magazines, comic books, etc.

Character sketches of relatives and friends

Descriptions of favorite authors, athletes, musicians, literary characters, etc.

PART II:
Relationships

Relationships

Objectives: To encourage students to think about the ways they interact and relate with others in their environments

To guide students in using their relationships with others in writing about their lives

Thinking Skills: Observation

Recall

Understanding

Application

Analysis

Divergent Thinking

Convergent Thinking

Synthesis

Evaluation

Directions: The four activities in "Relationships" need not be used in the sequence shown. Rearrange, delete, and add to suit the needs of your class.

Activity 16 should help children from combined and/or one-parent families understand that they are not different while giving them something to write about.

Activity 17 should help students broaden the meaning of friendship.

Activity 18 should help students understand the diversity and wealth in their own neighborhoods.

Activity 19 can be divided into three parts, or any one of the three parts can be used alone.

Family

A family is composed of people living together and functioning as a unit. Many people consider the ideal family to consist of a father, who works away from home; a mother, who stays at home; and two children, a boy and a girl. Well, that does **not** describe my family. Does it describe yours? If so, you are in a minority. There are as many interesting family situations as there are classmates in your classroom. In the space below write about your family. Do not forget to include grandparents and step-grandparents, aunts and uncles, parents and step-parents, and siblings—whole, half, and step.

MY FAMILY

_____

_____

_____

_____

_____

_____

_____

_____

_____

_____

_____

_____

_____

_____

_____

_____

_____

Friends

What is your definition of a friend? Who are your friends? Why are they your friends? Think of people older than you and younger than you who are your friends. Do you have friends who are relatives? In the space below write about a friend and the relationship you have with that friend.

A FRIEND

_____

_____

_____

_____

_____

_____

_____

_____

_____

_____

_____

_____

_____

_____

_____

_____

_____

_____

_____

_____

_____

The Folks in My Neighborhood

Whether you live in a mobile-home park, an apartment complex, a suburb, downtown, in a row home, in the country, in a small town, on the beach, in the mountains, in a mansion, or in some other situation, you still live in a neighborhood. A neighborhood is composed of the people living near each other; often the neighborhood has distinguishing characteristics, or a "personality" that has developed over a period of time. In this activity you will describe your neighborhood and your place in it. You might want to read Harper Lee's *To Kill a Mockingbird* for its emphasis on the importance of neighborhood.

Describe your neighborhood. How does it look? Include descriptions of streets, landscapes, buildings, views. How does it sound? How does it smell? Do sounds and smells change during a twenty-four-hour period? If so, how? How does it change from season to season?

_____

_____

_____

_____

How long have you lived in your neighborhood? How did you get to know various neighbors? Do your neighbors do anything together as a community (such as having a block party or raising money for charities)? Explain.

_____

_____

_____

Who are your closest neighbors? Include information about age, looks, ethnic backgrounds, religions, occupations, children, pets, hobbies, etc. What is your relationship with your neighbors? How does it vary from neighbor to neighbor? Why?

_____

_____

_____

_____

Heroes and Heroines

Activity No. 19

Student Work Sheet

There are many definitions of a hero/heroine. Among those are: A hero/heroine is a person admired for his/her achievements and outstanding character or a person who has shown great courage—either physical, mental, or moral. In this activity you will be writing about three kinds of heroes/heroines: people you know personally; historic, well-known personages (those who actually lived or are now living); and literary characters from books, movies, television, comic books, etc. First, identify the hero/heroine; second, tell what the person has done or achieved to make him/her heroic; and third, tell how the person's example has inspired or helped you.

A Hero/Heroine I Know:

_____

_____

_____

_____

_____

A Historic Hero/Heroine:

_____

_____

_____

_____

_____

A Literary Hero/Heroine:

_____

_____

_____

_____

_____

PART III:
The Future

The Future

Objectives: To encourage students to think about where they want their lives to go

To help students define "success"

To guide students in writing about their futures

Thinking Skills: Observation

Recall

Understanding

Application

Analysis

Divergent Thinking

Convergent Thinking

Synthesis

Evaluation

Directions: The six activities in "The Future" are designed to encourage students to think about where they want to go, what they hope to accomplish, and what they want to do and be in their lifetimes.

Activities 20 and 21 ask for concrete answers.

Activity 22 encourages students to free-wheel with their responses, to be creative and imaginative—even silly.

Activities 23 and 24 encourage idealistic responses. You might like to introduce a discussion of idealism and realism with this activity.

Activity 25 frightens some students, so it should be approached carefully. I have used it with gifted students and English students with amazing results. Encourage students to write their obits "their own way."

Scenario

A scenario is an account or synopsis of a projected course of action or events. In the following writing activity you will be making projections for various stages of your life. Think how old you will be at the various stages. What will your family situation be? What educational, professional, and personal goals will you have achieved by then?

Five years from now? _____

_____

_____

_____

Twenty years from now? _____

_____

_____

_____

Thirty-five years from now? _____

_____

_____

_____

Fifty years from now? _____

_____

_____

_____

Sixty years from now? _____

_____

_____

_____

Things I Like to Do

Activity No. 21

Student Work Sheet

In the space below list fifteen things you enjoy doing now. Next check the ten-year, thirty-year, and/or the fifty-year columns if you think you will still enjoy those things ten, thirty, and/or fifty years from now. What conclusions can you draw from the completed chart about your life?

Things I Enjoy Now	10 Years	30 Years	50 Years

Conclusions: _____

_____

_____

_____

Daydreams

Daydreaming allows people to circumvent human and natural limitations and explore the vast possibilities of life. What is your favorite daydream about your future? How does it transcend time, space, and your own personal limitations and allow you to become what you wish and do what you want? Write your favorite daydream below.

MY FAVORITE DAYDREAM

_____

_____

_____

_____

_____

_____

_____

_____

_____

_____

_____

_____

_____

_____

_____

_____

_____

_____

_____

_____

_____

Want Ads

Study the want ads in a newspaper. What does a good want ad do? Write want ads for the following:

A Future Spouse:

_____

_____

_____

Future Children:

_____

_____

_____

An Ideal Job:

_____

_____

_____

An Ideal Boss:

_____

_____

_____

Your Dream House:

_____

_____

_____

Others:

_____

_____

_____

Rules for Living

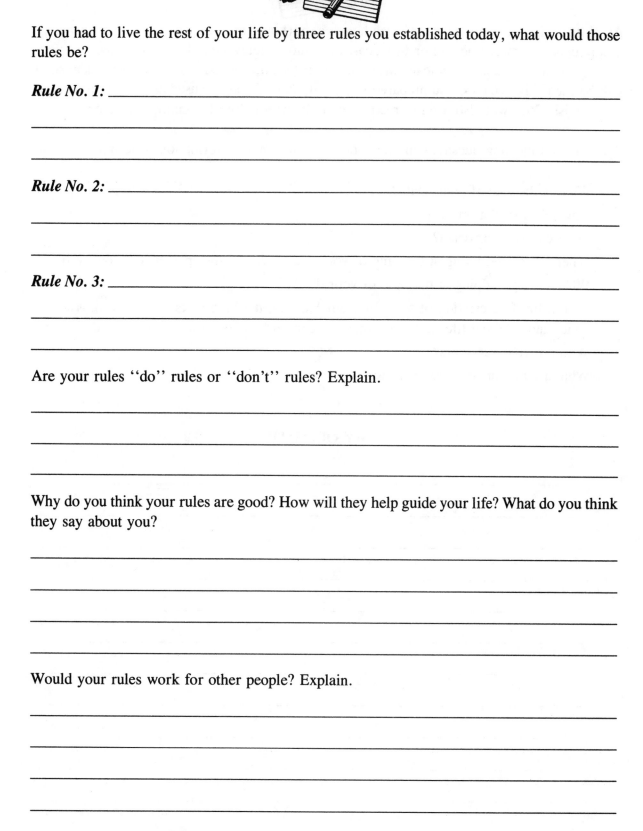

If you had to live the rest of your life by three rules you established today, what would those rules be?

Rule No. 1: _____

_____

_____

Rule No. 2: _____

_____

_____

Rule No. 3: _____

_____

_____

Are your rules "do" rules or "don't" rules? Explain.

_____

_____

_____

Why do you think your rules are good? How will they help guide your life? What do you think they say about you?

_____

_____

_____

_____

Would your rules work for other people? Explain.

_____

_____

_____

_____

Obituary

An obituary is a notice of a person's death with a short biographical account. It is published in a newspaper or magazine and/or broadcast on radio or television. In this exercise you will write your own obituary. Indicate which medium (radio, television, newspaper, magazine) will be used. The scenario you prepared in Activity No. 20 may be used as reference material if you wish. You will also need to read a few obituaries before beginning the activity.

Answer the following questions in your obituary. Add more information if desired.

What is the date of your death?

How old does that make you?

What caused your death?

Where were you living at the time of your death? What other places had you lived?

What were you doing at the time of your death?

Give a brief description of your life, emphasizing the highlights of your professional, civic, and personal life. List your major accomplishments, honors, and awards.

Who are your survivors?

What are the funeral arrangements?

MY OBITUARY

_____

_____

_____

_____

_____

_____

_____

_____

_____

_____

PART IV:
Autobiography

Autobiographies and Memoirs

Activity No. 26

Teacher Directions

Objectives: To guide students in writing longer papers

To encourage students to be selective in what they write

To teach students to condense and dramatize for the greatest effects in their writings

Thinking Skills: Observation

Recall

Understanding

Application

Analysis

Divergent Thinking

Convergent Thinking

Synthesis

Evaluation

Directions: Activity No. 26, "Autobiographies and Memoirs," asks students to write longer papers than the preceding twenty-five activities did; therefore, from one to two weeks should be devoted to this activity.

I always get better written, more interesting results from the topical autobiography than from the chronological form.

Autobiographies and Memoirs

A Typical Approach:

A typical approach to the topical autobiography would be to assign students three to five chapters. Students would write one chapter a day in class and then would use two class periods for revising and rewriting. Lengths of chapters would vary. Finally, students would share orally selected parts of their autobiographies. The best way of getting students started, I found, is to share some episodes from my own life with them and to show how I would write those episodes into my own autobiography.

FOR EXAMPLE:

CHAPTER 1: Self
Include personal descriptions, likes and dislikes, personality, values, motivations, achievements, hopes and dreams, future plans, etc.

CHAPTER 2: Family
Identify family members and tell about your relationship with each. What is your position and role in your family?

CHAPTER 3: An Important Person in My Life
Decide which person has had the greatest influence in your life. Describe that person, your relationship, and the impact of that relationship on your life.

CHAPTER 4: Other Topics
Choose a topic (or topics) from the list in the Activity No. 26 Student Work Sheets.

Autobiographies and Memoirs

Additional Information:

Whenever people write about their lives in their own words, they are writing autobiographies. Some autobiographers recount their lives from birth to the present. Others may describe their greatest adventure or several important periods in their lives. Regardless of what and how autobiographers choose to write, they all have one problem—they can seldom write an unbiased account of themselves. People who write their own life stories usually cannot be unpersonal, unemotional, and unbiased about their lives. Personal biases will, therefore, affect their interpretations. They have a tendency to present facts subjectively rather than objectively. It is only human to wish to appear in the best light possible.

Autobiographers cannot describe **everything** about their lives. They must select and condense their material into a readable account. One way of selecting and condensing material is to write about typical actions, personality traits, and settings. Another is to dramatize (show themselves speaking and acting) a few major and/or typical incidents in their lives.

Facts must also be kept straight. If students are in doubt about their facts, they should be expected to ascertain the correct information.

Research using old newspapers and magazines might be useful, especially the researching of newspapers printed on the day of birth.

You may wish to assign to students other autobiographies to be read and discussed before introducing the autobiography writing unit to them.

A WORD OF CAUTION: Sometimes confidentiality must be maintained. Sometimes the writing will be a request for help in dealing with a situation. You, as the teacher, must learn to tell the difference and act according to the individual situation.

Autobiographies and Memoirs

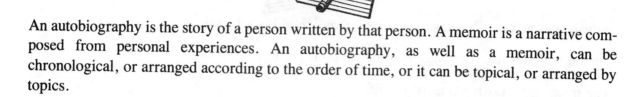

An autobiography is the story of a person written by that person. A memoir is a narrative composed from personal experiences. An autobiography, as well as a memoir, can be chronological, or arranged according to the order of time, or it can be topical, or arranged by topics.

Two important elements of autobiography are **selection**—what the narrators select to tell about themselves—and **condensation**—the way narrators choose to compress the myriad details of their lives into a readable account.

Choose the chronological style or the topical style and write your autobiography. You may wish to interview your parents and others about your early life. Appropriate snapshots or, if you have artistic ability, drawings would make your autobiography more interesting. Rewrite and include materials from other sections of this book when you can.

If you are writing a topical autobiography, some of the following topics might be useful to you:

Personal description

Personality

Likes and dislikes

Values

Motivations

Achievements

Hopes and dreams

Adjustment to a change (a move, a new stepparent, etc.)

Future plans

Family

The day I fell in love for the first time

Autobiographies and Memoirs

Advantages and disadvantages of being an only child or of having siblings

Person who has had the greatest influence on my life

The most embarrassing time of my life

The most exciting time of my life

The funniest time of my life

The saddest time of my life

The happiest time of my life

Hobbies and interests

Sports and games

My favorite daydream

A turning point (an incident that changed my life)

The role of religion in my life

Education

The best day of my life

The worst day of my life

A trip I'll never forget

My best friend

My grandparents (or other relatives)

Pets

Favorite TV show

Favorite Food

Autobiographies and Memoirs

Favorite book

Favorite author

The day I got my braces (glasses, contact lenses, etc.)

My mini-bike (go-cart, bike, roller blades, etc.)

A wedding (or other formal occasion) I attended and what happened

Why I collect _____

Taking tests

Favorite teacher

Favorite subject

Best party I ever attended

The day I learned to roller blade (ride my bike, drive, ski, swim, etc.)

Joke played on me

Joke I played on someone

My astrological sign and what it says about me

The most important discovery I have ever made and how it affected me

The hardest decision I ever made and how it affected my life

Fears and phobias and how they limit my life

Things I would change about myself if I could

Textures, tastes, smells, and sights I enjoy

Nightmares, dreams, and daydreams

Getting up in the morning

What happened in the rest of the world on the day I was born

Tear-out
Reproducible
Student
Work Pages

Mirror Image

Very few people know what they really look like to other people. In the following exercise you will describe yourself, starting at the top of your head and ending with your feet. You will need a full-length mirror and a hand mirror. Recent photographs may also be used. You may **not** ask anyone for help—you must determine the color of your hair, the color of your eyes, and the shape of your face yourself. Some characteristics are measurable; some will require a value judgment.

Name _____ Age _____ Sex _____

Height_____ Weight_____ Body Build_____

Hair Color _____ Texture _____ Style _____

Face Shape_____ Eye Color _____ Skin Color_____

Eyebrows _____ Nose _____ Mouth _____ Ears _____

Hand Shape _____ Ring Size _____ Fingernails _____

Arms _____ Legs _____

Foot Size _____ Shape _____

Distinguishing Marks _____

_____

Other Comments_____

_____

_____

What do you like best about your looks? Why?

_____

_____

_____

What do you like least about your looks? Why?

_____

_____

_____

Personality

What kind of personality do you have? Use the following set of questions as a guide to get you started; then add your own questions. You may use friends and family members to help you.

What kind of disposition do you have?

_____

_____

_____

What is your favorite time of day—the part of the day when you are most alert and productive and you feel the best?

_____

_____

How do you handle problems?

_____

_____

_____

Do you like a lot of friends or a few good ones? Explain.

_____

_____

_____

Do you like to work alone or with others? Explain.

_____

_____

_____

How do you get along with younger people? With older people? With your peers?

_____

_____

_____

Personality

What are your favorite activities? Explain.

_____

_____

_____

What peculiar traits, habits, or gestures are common to you?

_____

_____

_____

Do you have any phobias? If so, explain.

_____

_____

_____

What kind of speech do you use? Do you use slang? Explain. Do you have an accent? Explain.

_____

_____

_____

Are you the kind of person who likes to be independent, to do things your own way and at your own pace, or are you a ''crowd follower,'' one who goes along with whatever else the others want to do? Explain your answer.

_____

_____

_____

Other comments:

_____

_____

_____

Interview

In this activity you will interview yourself. First, read interviews and watch interviews on television. Notice how the best interviewers ask leading questions to direct their interviewees but allow the interviewees to do the majority of the talking. Also, notice how good interviewers are able to change focus or direction when the situation demands it. Second, answer the following questions: How could you make the interviews you read and watched better? What questions were not asked to which you wanted to know the answers? Third, construct your own questions, making them interesting and probing. Fourth, answer your questions thoroughly.

_____

_____

_____

_____

_____

_____

_____

_____

_____

_____

_____

_____

_____

_____

_____

_____

A Typical Day

So nothing ever happens to you, and you never have anything to write about? Hah! Don't you believe it. This activity will show you that in the normal course of a day things do happen that you can write about. Has today, so far, been a fairly typical day in your life? In this activity, you will write about **today.** Start at the beginning and work through the day detail by detail in chronological order, including where you went, what you ate, how you dressed, whom you saw, what was done, how you felt, and your reactions and thoughts.

A TYPICAL DAY IN MY LIFE

_____

_____

_____

_____

_____

_____

_____

_____

_____

_____

_____

_____

_____

_____

_____

_____

Famous Firsts

People seem to remember their "firsts." Choose one of the "firsts" listed below, or supply your own "first" and write a story about it.

My first party

My first birthday

My first Christmas

My first phone call

My first punishment

My first love

My first day of school

Other firsts: _____

_____

My first haircut

My first bicycle ride alone

My first date

My first pay check (or allowance)

My first visit to the dentist

My first visit to a restaurant

My first night away from home

Other firsts: _____

_____

MY FIRST _____

_____

_____

_____

_____

_____

_____

_____

_____

_____

_____

_____

_____

After School

What is your favorite after-school activity? What do you enjoy doing the most on weekends and after school is out during the week? In the space below, write a description of this activity (or activities) and tell why you enjoy it (them).

MY FAVORITE AFTER-SCHOOL ACTIVITY

_____

_____

_____

_____

_____

_____

_____

_____

_____

_____

_____

_____

_____

_____

_____

_____

_____

_____

When I Was Little

What was your life like when you were "little," before you started to go to school? How did you view the world? What were some misconceptions you had? What was a typical day like? What were your favorite games, toys, or people? You may need to interview others for some background information. If so, work the interview(s) into your account.

WHEN I WAS LITTLE

_____

_____

_____

_____

_____

_____

_____

_____

_____

_____

_____

_____

_____

_____

_____

_____

_____

_____

_____

_____

_____

Anecdotes

An anecdote is a short narrative of an interesting, amusing, and/or biographical incident. Refer to any issue of *Reader's Digest* and read "Humor in Uniform" or "Life in These United States" for examples of anecdotes. Analyze several anecdotes by answering the following questions: What do the anecdotes have in common? Why are they interesting and/or amusing? How is the humor achieved? How are the anecdotes different? Which is your favorite? Why? After you have analyzed several anecdotes, write your own. Remember, anecdotes are brief and to the point; however, you must include enough details so that your anecdote makes sense.

_____

_____

_____

_____

_____

_____

_____

_____

_____

_____

_____

_____

_____

_____

_____

_____

_____

_____

Wanted Posters

Choose one or more of the following and design wanted posters for them:

My ideal teacher

My ideal school

My ideal pet

My ideal neighbors

My ideal house or room

My ideal environment

My ideal vacation

Other ideals: _____

_____

_____

My ideal parents

My ideal best friend

My ideal sibling

My ideal neighborhood

My ideal food

My ideal day

My ideal trip

Other ideals: _____

_____

_____

WANTED: MY IDEAL _____

WANTED: MY IDEAL _____

Superstitions

Superstitions are beliefs and/or practices resulting from ignorance, fear of the unknown, trust in magic or chance, or a false conception of causation maintained despite evidence to the contrary. Regardless—black cats crossing my path make me uneasy; I knock on wood, cross my fingers, and make wishes at appropriate times. Do you practice any superstitions? Do you have a "lucky" object, a "lucky" outfit, or a "lucky" day of the week? In the space below write about a superstition and its effects on you.

MY SUPERSTITION

_____

_____

_____

_____

_____

_____

_____

_____

_____

_____

_____

_____

_____

_____

_____

_____

_____

_____

_____

Imaginary Friends

Many people have imaginary friends when they are very young; however, one of the most famous imaginary friends belonged to an adult. Elwood P. Dowd and his imaginary six-foot rabbit, Harvey, were made famous in the movie *Harvey,* which starred Jimmy Stewart as Dowd. Did you (or do you still) have imaginary friends? If so, who were (are) they? What did (do) they do? What happened to them if you no longer have them? In the space below write about your imaginary friend(s).

MY IMAGINARY FRIEND(S)

_____

_____

_____

_____

_____

_____

_____

_____

_____

_____

_____

_____

_____

_____

_____

_____

_____

_____

Activity No. 12

In this activity you are going to imaginatively remove all restraints in your life and let your creativity determine what your life would be like if you could live anywhere you wanted, be anything you wanted, and do anything you wanted, whenever you wanted—well, you get the drift, I'm sure. So, give it a try.

If I could live anywhere and any way I wanted, I would _____

_____

_____

_____

_____

_____

_____

If I could be anything I wanted, I would _____

_____

_____

_____

_____

_____

_____

If I could do anything I wanted, whenever I wanted, I would _____

_____

_____

_____

_____

_____

_____

Role Reversal

What would it be like for you to change places with someone for a while? In Mark Twain's *The Prince and the Pauper* the prince and the pauper changed places for a time. In Mary Rodgers' *Freaky Friday* a mother and a daughter changed personalities. In *The Whipping Boy* the prince and his whipping boy were mistaken for each other. What would happen if you became your teacher, your parent, your dog, or your best friend? Choose something or someone you would like to be for a short period of time. Write about what would happen and how you would feel if you could reverse roles.

WHEN I SWITCHED ROLES WITH _____

_____

_____

_____

_____

_____

_____

_____

_____

_____

_____

_____

_____

_____

_____

_____

_____

_____

_____

And the Winner Is...

You have just won $50,000 on a game show. The $50,000 must be spent within a twenty-four-hour period. It cannot be saved or invested. How will you spend your money?

MONEY TO SPEND

_____

_____

_____

_____

_____

_____

_____

_____

_____

_____

_____

_____

_____

_____

_____

_____

_____

_____

Journals and Diaries

Activity No. 15

You can create your own written history by keeping a journal or a diary. A journal or a diary is an account of events, transactions, or observations or a record of experiences, ideas, or reflections kept regularly for private use. Journal or diary entries should always be dated with the day, the month, and the year given. The place of writing should also be noted. You can purchase diaries and journals or you can make your own using notebooks. Many writers prefer to use loose-leaf notebooks because they can make the entries as long as they wish in them.

Start to keep a diary or journal. Be sure to write about typical days and events as well as unusual ones. You will probably want to include some of the topics listed below.

Where I go

What I do

Whom I see

What I say

What they say

How I feel about _____

My reaction(s) to _____

Plans

Current events

What's popular in music, dance, dress, slang, TV, movies, magazines, comic books, etc.

Character sketches of relatives and friends

Descriptions of favorite authors, athletes, musicians, literary characters, etc.

Family

A family is composed of people living together and functioning as a unit. Many people consider the ideal family to consist of a father, who works away from home; a mother, who stays at home; and two children, a boy and a girl. Well, that does **not** describe my family. Does it describe yours? If so, you are in a minority. There are as many interesting family situations as there are classmates in your classroom. In the space below write about your family. Do not forget to include grandparents and step-grandparents, aunts and uncles, parents and step-parents, and siblings—whole, half, and step.

MY FAMILY

_____

_____

_____

_____

_____

_____

_____

_____

_____

_____

_____

_____

_____

_____

_____

_____

_____

Friends

What is your definition of a friend? Who are your friends? Why are they your friends? Think of people older than you and younger than you who are your friends. Do you have friends who are relatives? In the space below write about a friend and the relationship you have with that friend.

A FRIEND

_____

_____

_____

_____

_____

_____

_____

_____

_____

_____

_____

_____

_____

_____

_____

_____

_____

_____

_____

The Folks in My Neighborhood

Activity No. 18

Whether you live in a mobile-home park, an apartment complex, a suburb, downtown, in a row home, in the country, in a small town, on the beach, in the mountains, in a mansion, or in some other situation, you still live in a neighborhood. A neighborhood is composed of the people living near each other; often the neighborhood has distinguishing characteristics, or a ''personality'' that has developed over a period of time. In this activity you will describe your neighborhood and your place in it. You might want to read Harper Lee's *To Kill a Mockingbird* for its emphasis on the importance of neighborhood.

Describe your neighborhood. How does it look? Include descriptions of streets, landscapes, buildings, views. How does it sound? How does it smell? Do sounds and smells change during a twenty-four-hour period? If so, how? How does it change from season to season?

_____

_____

_____

_____

_____

How long have you lived in your neighborhood? How did you get to know various neighbors? Do your neighbors do anything together as a community (such as having a block party or raising money for charities)? Explain.

_____

_____

_____

_____

Who are your closest neighbors? Include information about age, looks, ethnic backgrounds, religions, occupations, children, pets, hobbies, etc. What is your relationship with your neighbors? How does it vary from neighbor to neighbor? Why?

_____

_____

_____

_____

Heroes and Heroines

There are many definitions of a hero/heroine. Among those are: A hero/heroine is a person admired for his/her achievements and outstanding character or a person who has shown great courage—either physical, mental, or moral. In this activity you will be writing about three kinds of heroes/heroines: people you know personally; historic, well-known personages (those who actually lived or are now living); and literary characters from books, movies, television, comic books, etc. First, identify the hero/heroine; second, tell what the person has done or achieved to make him/her heroic; and third, tell how the person's example has inspired or helped you.

A Hero/Heroine I Know:

_____

_____

_____

_____

_____

A Historic Hero/Heroine:

_____

_____

_____

_____

_____

A Literary Hero/Heroine:

_____

_____

_____

_____

_____

Scenario

A scenario is an account or synopsis of a projected course of action or events. In the following writing activity you will be making projections for various stages of your life. Think how old you will be at the various stages. What will your family situation be? What educational, professional, and personal goals will you have achieved by then?

Five years from now? _____

_____

_____

_____

Twenty years from now? _____

_____

_____

_____

Thirty-five years from now? _____

_____

_____

_____

Fifty years from now? _____

_____

_____

_____

Sixty years from now? _____

_____

_____

_____

Things I Like to Do

Activity No. 21

Student Work Sheet

In the space below list fifteen things you enjoy doing now. Next check the ten-year, thirty-year, and/or the fifty-year columns if you think you will still enjoy those things ten, thirty, and/or fifty years from now. What conclusions can you draw from the completed chart about your life?

Things I Enjoy Now	10 Years	30 Years	50 Years

Conclusions: _____

_____

_____

_____

Daydreams

Daydreaming allows people to circumvent human and natural limitations and explore the vast possibilities of life. What is your favorite daydream about your future? How does it transcend time, space, and your own personal limitations and allow you to become what you wish and do what you want? Write your favorite daydream below.

MY FAVORITE DAYDREAM

_____

_____

_____

_____

_____

_____

_____

_____

_____

_____

_____

_____

_____

_____

_____

_____

_____

_____

Want Ads

Activity No. 23

Study the want ads in a newspaper. What does a good want ad do? Write want ads for the following:

A Future Spouse:

_____

_____

_____

Future Children:

_____

_____

_____

An Ideal Job:

_____

_____

_____

An Ideal Boss:

_____

_____

_____

Your Dream House:

_____

_____

_____

Others:

_____

_____

_____

Rules for Living

If you had to live the rest of your life by three rules you established today, what would those rules be?

Rule No. 1: _____

_____

_____

Rule No. 2: _____

_____

_____

Rule No. 3: _____

_____

_____

Are your rules ''do'' rules or ''don't'' rules? Explain.

_____

_____

_____

Why do you think your rules are good? How will they help guide your life? What do you think they say about you?

_____

_____

_____

_____

Would your rules work for other people? Explain.

_____

_____

_____

_____

Obituary

An obituary is a notice of a person's death with a short biographical account. It is published in a newspaper or magazine and/or broadcast on radio or television. In this exercise you will write your own obituary. Indicate which medium (radio, television, newspaper, magazine) will be used. The scenario you prepared in Activity No. 20 may be used as reference material if you wish. You will also need to read a few obituaries before beginning the activity.

Answer the following questions in your obituary. Add more information if desired.

> What is the date of your death?
>
> How old does that make you?
>
> What caused your death?
>
> Where were you living at the time of your death? What other places had you lived?
>
> What were you doing at the time of your death?
>
> Give a brief description of your life, emphasizing the highlights of your professional, civic, and personal life. List your major accomplishments, honors, and awards.
>
> Who are your survivors?
>
> What are the funeral arrangements?

MY OBITUARY

_____

_____

_____

_____

_____

_____

_____

_____

_____

_____

Autobiographies and Memoirs

Activity No. 26

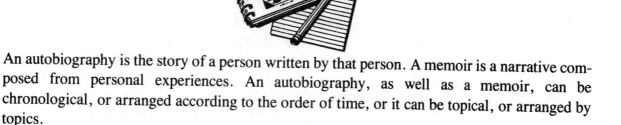

An autobiography is the story of a person written by that person. A memoir is a narrative composed from personal experiences. An autobiography, as well as a memoir, can be chronological, or arranged according to the order of time, or it can be topical, or arranged by topics.

Two important elements of autobiography are **selection**—what the narrators select to tell about themselves—and **condensation**—the way narrators choose to compress the myriad details of their lives into a readable account.

Choose the chronological style or the topical style and write your autobiography. You may wish to interview your parents and others about your early life. Appropriate snapshots or, if you have artistic ability, drawings would make your autobiography more interesting. Rewrite and include materials from other sections of this book when you can.

If you are writing a topical autobiography, some of the following topics might be useful to you:

Personal description

Personality

Likes and dislikes

Values

Motivations

Achievements

Hopes and dreams

Adjustment to a change (a move, a new stepparent, etc.)

Future plans

Family

The day I fell in love for the first time

Autobiographies and Memoirs

Advantages and disadvantages of being an only child or of having siblings

Person who has had the greatest influence on my life

The most embarrassing time of my life

The most exciting time of my life

The funniest time of my life

The saddest time of my life

The happiest time of my life

Hobbies and interests

Sports and games

My favorite daydream

A turning point (an incident that changed my life)

The role of religion in my life

Education

The best day of my life

The worst day of my life

A trip I'll never forget

My best friend

My grandparents (or other relatives)

Pets

Favorite TV show

Favorite Food

Autobiographies and Memoirs

Favorite book

Favorite author

The day I got my braces (glasses, contact lenses, etc.)

My mini-bike (go-cart, bike, roller blades, etc.)

A wedding (or other formal occasion) I attended and what happened

Why I collect _____

Taking tests

Favorite teacher

Favorite subject

Best party I ever attended

The day I learned to roller blade (ride my bike, drive, ski, swim, etc.)

Joke played on me

Joke I played on someone

My astrological sign and what it says about me

The most important discovery I have ever made and how it affected me

The hardest decision I ever made and how it affected my life

Fears and phobias and how they limit my life

Things I would change about myself if I could

Textures, tastes, smells, and sights I enjoy

Nightmares, dreams, and daydreams

Getting up in the morning

What happened in the rest of the world on the day I was born